At the Lake in June

Story by Suzanne Barchers
Illustrated by Randy Chewning
Designed and Produced by Six Red Marbles

June is here at last. The sun is so hot.

Say It   Sound It   Spell It

June is here at last. The sun is so hot.

Say It   Sound It   Spell It

 "Let's go to the lake!" says Jude. "We like it a lot!"

"Can Duke go, too?" says Luke. "He will have such fun."

Say It   Sound It   Spell It

 Duke likes to run over the huge dunes and then nap in the sun.

GO

"You know the rules!" says Mom. "First, get your chores done."

Say It   Sound It   Spell It

"Let's clean up this mess. Then we can go have fun."

Luke has a huge job. But Jude helps him, too.

Say It   Sound It   Spell It

Even Duke helps. There's lots he can do.

 Jude has a cute suit. Luke gets a huge tube.

Say It   Sound It   Spell It

Mom fixes snacks.
Even Duke will
want food!

GO

They pack up the car. Duke gets in the back.

Say It   Sound It   Spell It

Luke sits next to Duke, and Jude puts in the snack.

GO

As they ride to the lake, Luke and Jude sing a cute tune.

Say It   Sound It   Spell It

In no time at all, they see the lake and sand dunes.

GO

Jude grabs her raft. Luke uses his tube.

Say It   Sound It   Spell It

Duke runs for the dunes. Mom pours juice and adds ice cubes.

Dad sings a tune as he strums on his lute.

Say It   Sound It   Spell It

Mom hums the tune and then plays on her flute.

GO "It's snack time," says Mom.
"Let's sit here," says Luke.

Say It   Sound It   Spell It

"No, I want to sit there," says Jude. "Come on, Duke."

They all look at
Dad. He says, "I
will not have a
dispute."

Say It   Sound It   Spell It

"Okay," say Jude and Luke as they give Dad a salute.

It's time to go on this fine day in June. They wave goodbye as Duke howls a tune.

Say It   Sound It   Spell It

 Let's learn some more!

pole

dune

rope

flute

lute

tune

Jude

Luke

slope

bone

nose

tube

cone

robe